Nana Knows: Nana's Helping Hand With PTSD

A Unique Nurturing Perspective to Empowering Children Against a Life-Altering Impact

Workbook

By

Anita Miranda
MAEd, USNR

Illustrated By

Samantha Leiter

Nana Knows Series
Nana's Helping Hand With PTSD
A Unique Nurturing Perspective to Empowering
Children Against a Life-Altering Impact
Workbook

Living Disabled Publishing
Publication Date: 2015
First Edition, 2015
2015© Miranda's Creatives, LLC. All Rights Reserved
Printed in USA
1098765 4321

Hard Cover ISBN: 978-0692452479
Paperback ISBN: 978-0692461884
Workbook ISBN: 978-0692450956

Free Gift
with the purchase
of this book

30 Minute Private,
One-on-One Mentoring
Session

NanaKnowsSeries.com

Edited & Illustrated by: Samantha Leiter
Assistant Editor: Hortencia Gardea
Design, Layout, and Graphics Design: Samantha Leiter & Anita Miranda
Cover Design: Samantha Leiter & Anita Miranda

Contact the Author:
Anita Miranda: LivingDisabled@gmail.com
www.LivingDisabledNOTDead.com

This book belongs to:

_____

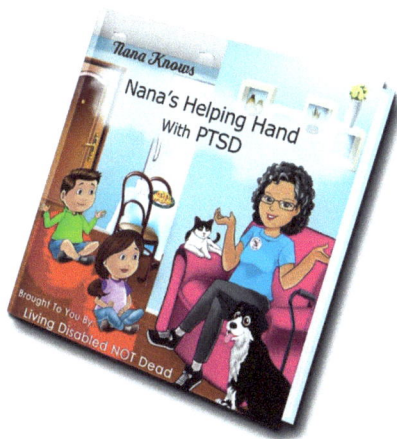

and I am ___ years old.

I live in the State of _____.

My _____ gave me this book.

With Love,

_____

This is My Family
Complete the Drawing

Proceeds Benefits Circle Of Helping Hands, 501(c)(3)

I feel bad when

_____

_____

_____

_____

_____

_____

_____

_____

I am happy when

I feel confused when

_____

- - - - - - - - - - - - - - - - - - -

_____

- - - - - - - - - - - - - - - - - - -

_____

_____

_____

- - - - - - - - - - - - - - - - - - -

_____

- - - - - - - - - - - - - - - - - - -

_____

Oh Oh! I made

Proceeds Benefits Circle Of Helping Hands, 501(c)(3)

This makes me mad

_____
- -
_____

_____
- -
_____

_____
- -
_____

_____
- -
_____

I like when

_____
- -
_____
- -
_____
- -
_____
- -
_____
- -
_____
- -
_____

I am scared because

Did I do that?

I wish my parents

If I had super powers

_____

- - - - - - - - - - - - - - - - - -

_____

- - - - - - - - - - - - - - - - - -

_____

- - - - - - - - - - - - - - - - - -

_____

- - - - - - - - - - - - - - - - - -

_____

- - - - - - - - - - - - - - - - - -

_____

- - - - - - - - - - - - - - - - - -

_____

- - - - - - - - - - - - - - - - - -

_____

Proceeds Benefits Circle Of Helping Hands, 501(c)(3)

Who is Nana?

_____
- -

What is she doing?

_____
- -

Who comes to visit?

_____
- -

Who is crying? & Who is mad?

_____
- -

_____
- -

Circle One

Nana offered:

1. Milk & Chips
2. Milk & Cookies
3. Cookies & Water

Bella takes out:

1. Comfy chairs
2. Stools
3. Beanbags

The cat and dog's names are:

1. Jennifer & Jack
2. Jenny & Jack
3. Jill & Jack

Proceeds Benefits Circle Of Helping Hands, 501(c)(3)

In the beginning what are
the twins doing?

What pops into Nana's head?

Nana's mom looked like a:

What happens on a bad day?

Circle One

What was Bobby doing that woke Mom up:

1. Watching Tv
2. Playing with Dinosaurs
3. Taking a bath

When Mom yelled at Bobby:

1. He cried
2. He took a nap
3. He laughed

Proceeds Benefits Circle Of Helping Hands, 501(c)(3)

Who was sorry that Bobby got scared?

Who was strong for Bobby?

When Nana grew up, she joined?

Nana's mom was?

Something bad has happened...
Share something bad that has
happened to you or someone you know.

If something bad happens
I can talk to:

_____

_____

I have a safe place to go to.
Draw here.

I pretend that:

_____

- -

This is my house. Please draw.

I feel like this right now? Circle 1.

Proceeds Benefits Circle Of Helping Hands, 501(c)(3)

September 11 (9/11) means what to you?

_____

_____

Can you draw a picture of 9/11?

What is a trauma?

_____

_____

_____

_____

A flashback is like a what?

___

When Bobby & Bella were watching a movie, who got mad?

___

Why?

___

What would you do if that happened to you?

___

Proceeds Benefits Circle Of Helping Hands, 501(c)(3)

Circle One

Bobby asked if Nana was:

1. Going for a drive
2. Baking cookies
3. Sick

Nana said:

1. I have the flu
2. I have PTSD
3. I am sad

True or False

Only military people get PTSD

○ True
○ False

Anyone from kids to adults can get PtSD

○ True
○ False

P stands for?

_ _ _ _ _ _ _ _ _ _ _ _ _ _

T stands for?

_ _ _ _ _ _ _ _ _ _ _ _ _ _

S stands for?

_ _ _ _ _ _ _ _ _ _ _ _ _ _

D stands for?

_ _ _ _ _ _ _ _ _ _ _ _ _ _

Shock absorbers do what for a car?

Homework.
Next time you ride in a car close your eyes.
Does your car have good shock absorbers?

Name 3 symptoms of PTSD?

What stresses you out?

_____

- -

Do you feel stressed in the morning or in the evening?

_____

- -

Name 3 things that can cause stress?

_____

- -

_____

_____

- -

True or False

PTSD can go away

○ True
○ False

PTSD can be managed

○ True
○ False

It is my fault

○ True
○ False

This is how I can help?

A time out is not
always a bad thing.

○ True
○ False

Words/Phrases to Avoid

It is all in your head
What's wrong with you anyway
Crazy...
It is not that big of a deal
Why are you causing a fuss
Your...probably caused it anyway
I should have left
I never should have...
This is not a good time...
Get over it
Do you have to do this now
It isn't all about you
No one is going to put up with you

These phrases are my personal triggers, when I hear any of these during a flashback, I tend to fall deeper into the spiraling emotion. I learned through therapy and my own recovery to share with those who love and have any interaction with me my list.

Use this time to talk to a therapist and/or parent to find your loved ones "trigger words" to avoid.
~Nana

Words to Avoid
Write Your Own

Positive Safe Words

I am here
I am not leaving
We are in this together
It is not your fault
You did not do anything bad
I still love you
We are a family
This too shall pass
I believe you
I can see why you feel this way

These phrases are what I learned through therapy and my own recovery.
Use this time to talk to a therapist and/or parent
to find your special positive safe words.
~Nana

Positive Safe Words
Write Your Own

_____

- - - - - - - - - - - - - - - - - - -

_____

- - - - - - - - - - - - - - - - - - -

_____

- - - - - - - - - - - - - - - - - - -

_____

- - - - - - - - - - - - - - - - - - -

_____

- - - - - - - - - - - - - - - - - - -

_____

- - - - - - - - - - - - - - - - - - -

_____

- - - - - - - - - - - - - - - - - - -

_____

How does Nana Know?

- -

- -

There is alot of what and what going on in Bella and Bobby's home?

- -

I feel like this right now? Circle 1.

www.ingramcontent.com/pod-product-compliance
Lightning Source LLC
Chambersburg PA
CBHW042104040426
42448CB00002B/130